A Kid's Guide to Drawing™

How to Draw
Fish

Justin Lee

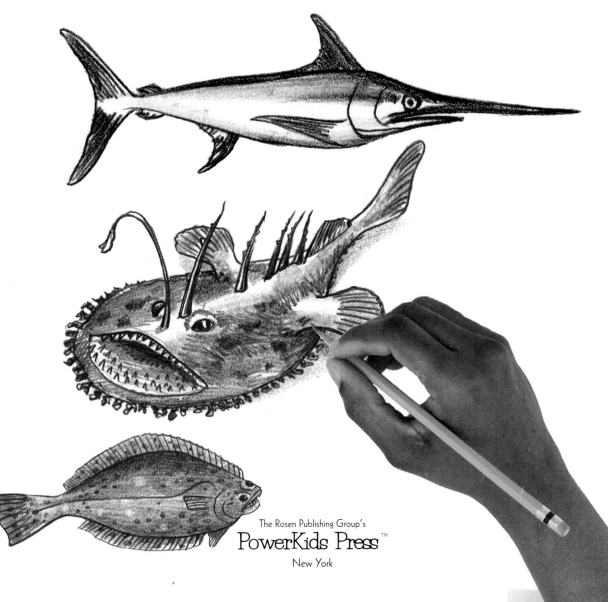

The Rosen Publishing Group's
PowerKids Press™
New York

We don't know everything about fish, but we know that they are beautiful.
This book is for my brother Colin who is beautiful as well as mysterious.

Published in 2002 by The Rosen Publishing Group, Inc.
29 East 21st Street, New York, NY 10010

This work is adapted from the book Draw Ocean Animals—A Step by Step Guide with illustrations and instructions by Doug DuBosque, which was published by Peel Productions, Inc. Copyright © 1994 Douglas C. DuBosque. All rights reserved.

First Edition

Book Design: Kim Sonsky
Layout: Michael Caroleo
Project Editor: Frances E. Ruffin

Photo Credits: p. 6 © Scott Kerrigan/CORBIS; p. 8 © Robert Yin/CORBIS; p. 10 © Peter Renyolds; Frank Lane Picture Agency/CORBIS; pp. 12, 18 © Stephen Frink/CORBIS; p. 14 © Amos Nachoum/CORBIS; p. 16 © Brandon D. Cole/CORBIS; p. 20 © Tom Brakefield/CORBIS.

Lee, Justin, 1973–
    How to Draw Fish / Justin Lee.— 1st ed.
        p. cm. — (A kid's guide to drawing)
Includes index.
    ISBN 0-8239-5792-6
    1. Fishes in art—Juvenile literature. 2. Drawing—Technique—Juvenile literature. [1. Fishes in art. 2. Drawing—Technique.]
I. Title. II. Series.
    NC781 .L439 2002
    743.6'7—dc21

                                                                          00-012298

Manufactured in the United States of America

CONTENTS

Let's Draw Fish

Have you ever stared into a fish tank and watched the fish swim smoothly through the water? It is easy to be amazed by their sparkling scales and powerful tails.

There are more than 20,000 different **species** of fish. They can be very different, from the goldfish to the giant moray eel found in ocean waters. There are three main types of fish. One type includes ancient, jawless fish. There are only two species of jawless fish left in the world. Boneless fish, such as sharks, are a second type. The third type of fish is the bony fish. They make up most of the world's fish. These are the fish we are going to study.

All bony fish have fins and jaws. All fish get their **oxygen** from the water, but a few fish also can breathe air. Most fish have scales that protect their skin like armor. Their scales can be many different colors and shapes. Some fish eat plants, some eat animals, and some eat whatever they can find. Some fish, such as the lionfish, are poisonous, and others, such as the angler fish, hide and wait for their **prey**. Still other fish depend on speed and strength to catch their dinner.

There are many interesting things to learn about fish. One great way to learn about fish is to draw them. Here is a list of supplies that you will need to draw fish:

- A sketch pad
- A number 2 pencil
- A pencil sharpener
- An eraser

You can learn to draw each fish in a few short steps. All of the drawings begin with a few simple shapes. From there you will add other shapes and details. The drawing terms for the basic shapes that you will need to draw fish are listed on page 22.

Some people can draw right away, and others need more practice. If you need a little practice, don't give up. Your drawings will be your own special creations, and the more practice you have, the better your drawings will be.

Swordfish

Swordfish have a long, bony sword on the front of their heads, but no teeth! Swordfish live in deep, warm water all over the world. They can grow up to 15 feet (4.6 m) and can weigh 1,300 pounds (590 kg). They are powerful fish that can travel up to 60 miles per hour (100 km/h). They swim so fast that they sometimes run into boats and get their swords stuck.

Baby swordfish don't have swords. As they become adults, they lose their scales and develop a sword. Adult swordfish are dark on top and light on their bellies. This coloring makes it hard to see them from above or beneath. Swordfish's big eyes help them see as they swim through the water, looking for fish, crabs, shrimp, and other food.

1

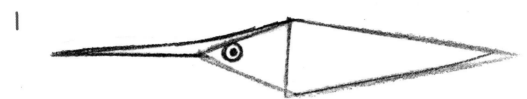

Draw two triangles for the body. The sword is part of the upper jaw, so draw it attached to the top of the small triangle. Add the eye.

2

Next draw the dorsal fin and the lower jaw.

3

Add the other fins and round out the body shape.

4

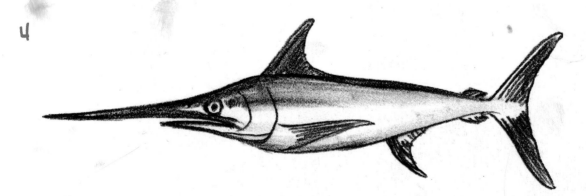

Add shading. Sharpen outlines and details. Clean up any smudges with your eraser.

Butterfly Fish

Butterfly fish look like small, colorful saucers. Most butterfly fish only reach a size of about 6 inches (15.2 cm) in length. They live in warm, shallow water in and around the **coral reefs** of the world. Butterfly fish's bright colors help to disguise them. This may seem odd, but in a coral reef there is so much color that being bright actually makes it easier to hide. Most butterfly fish have a dark spot on their tail. The dark spot looks like an eye. Scientists believe that this false eye confuses other animals, making it easier for the butterfly fish to catch their prey. Butterfly fish eat small animals that live in the coral reef. They also like to eat the **tentacles** off small sea worms.

1

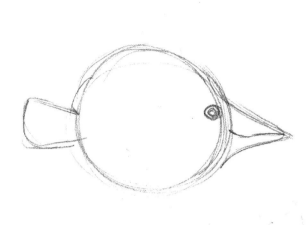

Start with a light circle. At one end, add the tail. At the other end, draw the long, beaklike snout. Add a line for the mouth. Draw the eye.

2

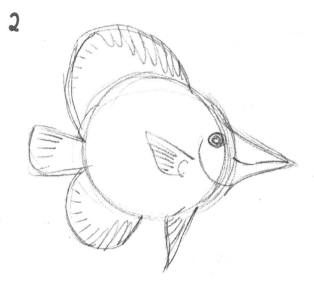

Your next challenge is to draw all the fins with spines. Five fins are visible in this drawing. Draw them all!

3

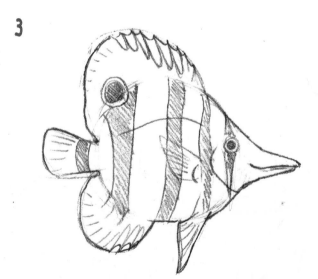

Next add the camouflage pattern, including the second eye to fool attackers.

4

Darken the patterns. The eye and band on the tail are black. The stripes are copper colored. Sharpen outlines and details. Clean up with your eraser.

Angler Fish

The angler fish is flat and round and has a huge mouth. An angler has a long **spine** that sticks out of its head. This spine looks to other fish like food hanging in the water. When other fish swim by, the angler fish opens its huge mouth and sucks in its prey.

The angler fish usually lies on the bottom of the ocean. Its brownish gray skin blends into the ocean floor. Small pieces of skin hang in little flaps all over its body. The flaps of skin on the angler fish make it hard for other animals to see it.

The angler fish is a deep-water animal. It prefers to live in water about 1,800 feet (549 m) deep. It can grow to be 6 feet (1.8 m) long. It eats any animal that comes close enough to its lure. The only animal that eats the angler fish is the huge sperm whale.

1

Draw a flat oval, with an arc across the top of it for the centerline of the fish's body. Draw the rough outline of the tail.

2

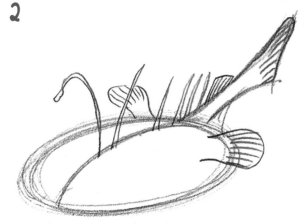

Along the centerline (start back far enough to leave room for the mouth!) draw the "fishing rod" and other dorsal spines. Add the pectoral fins and tail details.

3

Draw the mouth with teeth. Add eyes. Draw lightly at first! Now comes the part requiring patience—slowly draw the frills around the outside edge. Do a little bit at a time, erasing part of the oval as you draw.

4

Add shading. Sharpen outlines and details. Clean up any smudges with your eraser.

Moray Eel

The moray eel spends its days hiding in the rocks and reefs of warm, shallow waters. It is a long, thin animal that looks like a thick snake. The moray eel doesn't swim like a fish. Instead, it slithers like a snake. Its body is covered in a thick skin that constantly produces a slimy substance. This makes it easier for the eel to slide through the water.

There are more than 100 different species of moray eels. We are going to draw the California moray, which lives along the coast of Southern California and Mexico. It grows up to 5 feet (1.5 m) long and has powerful jaws that it uses to catch and devour its prey. California morays feed on crabs, shrimps, lobsters, and other fish.

1

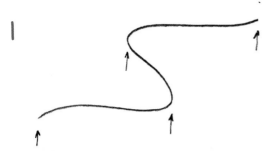

Start with a curved line.

2

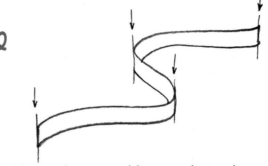

Add straight, vertical lines at the ends and at the curves. Hold your pencil flat on the paper if you have trouble seeing how to draw the vertical lines. Add more curved lines beneath the first ones, connecting to the vertical lines. See how the line turns into a ribbon?

3

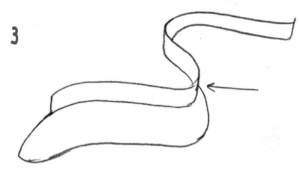

You may need a few tries to figure out the next few steps, so draw lightly at first! Pay special attention to the arrows. From the left side of the ribbon, draw a sausage shape, with your line ending at the arrow.

4

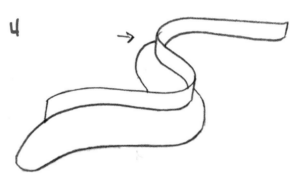

Draw a small line to make the second part of the body.

5

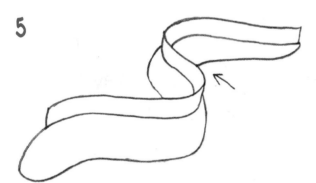

Add a third line. Now you've drawn the entire body of the eel. Take a moment to look at your drawing. Does it look like it's swimming toward you?

6

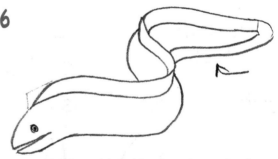

Next add the ribbonlike fin along the bottom of the eel. Draw the mouth and the eye. Add an angle to the front of the dorsal fin.

7

Add shading and spots. Clean up any smudges with your eraser.

Lionfish

The lionfish is brightly colored with stripes of orange, brown, and white. It lives in the coral reefs of the Indo-Pacific Ocean.

The lionfish has **venom** in its spines. If an animal comes close enough to touch a lionfish, it will get stung. The venom is strong enough to kill animals larger than itself. When a lionfish feels threatened, it raises its **dorsal fins**. This makes it look bigger than it really is. The fins also resemble a lion's mane. If the attacker doesn't leave, the lionfish will swim toward it with its spines out, ready to sting.

The lionfish does not use its poison to catch its food. A lionfish swims slowly through the **coral** and rock, looking for food to eat. It eats small fish and anything else it can catch and devour. Lionfish sometimes hunt in groups.

1

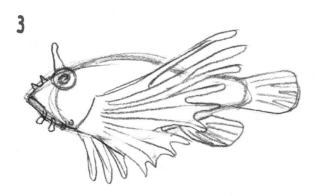

Start with a simple, oval shape. Add a rounded part for the tail at one end, and a point at the other. Draw the eye. Notice where it lies on the oval.

2

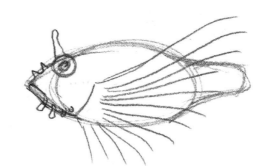

Add a line for the mouth, barbels on the chin, and the "eyebrow" above the eye. Lightly draw radiating curved lines for the spines of the pectoral fin.

3

Complete the pectoral fin. Add the caudal (tail) fin and anal fin. Erase any body lines that you no longer need.

4

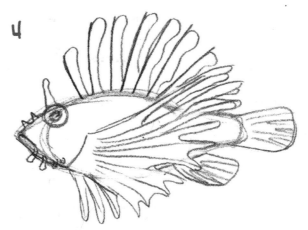

Add the large dorsal fin, which is in many parts. At the front of each part is a spine.

5

To sharpen the lines, you can go over outlines and important details with a fine marker. Clean up with your eraser.

California Halibut

California halibut live on the soft, sandy ocean bottom along California's coast. They won't live in water deeper than 600 feet (183 m).

California halibut are large, flat fish with both eyes on one side of their head. When the California halibut is young, though, it has an eye on each side of its head. As it grows older, one eye starts to move. Eventually both eyes of the halibut will be on the same side of its head. The halibut can change color to match its surroundings and is almost invisible when it lies on the ocean floor. The halibut lies there with just its eyes sticking out of the mud. When fish swim over it, the halibut quickly comes out of its hiding place and swallows its prey.

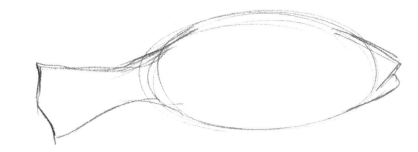

Draw an oval, with one end pointed. Draw the mouth. Add the tail.

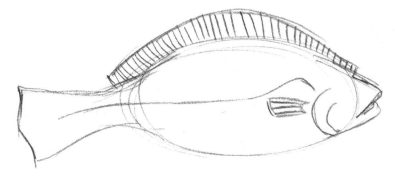

Draw the dorsal fin with spines. Draw the lateral line, pectoral fin, and gill openings.

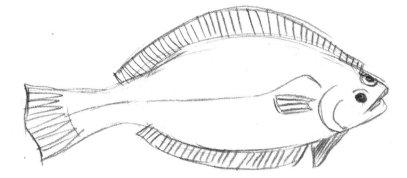

Add the two separate fins on the bottom. Draw the eyes. Add spines in the tail. Lightly erase lines that you don't need.

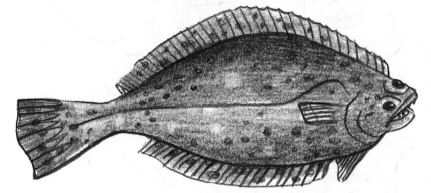

Add shading and spots. Sharpen outlines and details. Clean up any smudges with your eraser.

Parrotfish

Parrotfish get their name because their mouth looks like a parrot's beak. They have two large front teeth that are stuck together to help them chip **algae** and other plants off the hard coral. Parrotfish live in warm-water coral reefs around the world. They only eat ocean plants. They don't live in deep water because few plants grow there. Many scuba divers like to watch these fish because they are so pretty and are active in the daytime.

There are many different kinds of parrotfish. We are going to draw the rainbow parrotfish. It is a greenish blue color. Sometimes, as it gets older, it turns brownish orange. Its teeth are a bluish green! These fish can grow up to 4 feet (1.2 m) long.

1

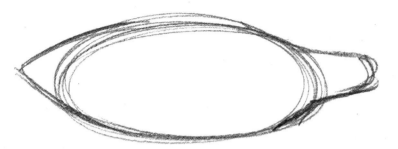

Start with a long oval. Add a point at one end and a rounded shape for a tail at the other.

2

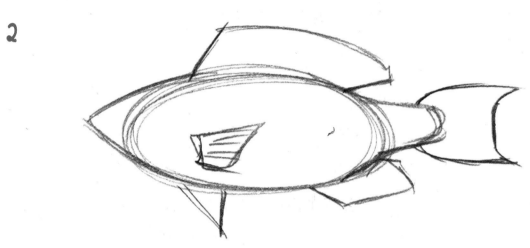

Add the dorsal fin. Next draw the pectoral fin. Add the pelvic, anal, and tail fins.

3

Draw the mouth, eye, and gill openings. Add scales, spines in the fins, and shading. Sharpen outlines and details. Clean up any smudges with your eraser.

Queen Triggerfish

Triggerfish have three spines on the top of their back. These spines can be folded down, then released quickly, like a trigger. This action makes the triggerfish look bigger than it is and scares other fish.

We are going to draw the queen triggerfish. This fish is very brightly colored. It has bright blue and purple stripes on its body, and fins and a starburst around its eyes. It lives in warm coral reefs where there is a lot of color, so its brightness helps it blend in. The queen triggerfish also can change color to blend into its background. Queen triggerfish can grow up to 2 feet (0.6 m) long. They eat crabs, coral, octopus, and sea urchins.

1

Draw a tilted oval. Add the jaws and the mouth. Extend the bottom jaw to make the body slightly pointed at the bottom. Draw a small shape for the base of the tail.

2

Draw the eye. Notice how far back it is from the mouth. Add the pectoral fin. Draw the first dorsal fin with spines. Behind it, draw the long, pointed, second dorsal fin.

3

Draw the caudal (tail) fin and the anal fin. Erase the parts of the oval that you no longer need.

4

Add stripes, patterns on fins, scales, and other details. Clean up any smudges with your eraser.

Drawing Terms

Here are some of the words and shapes that you will need to draw fish:

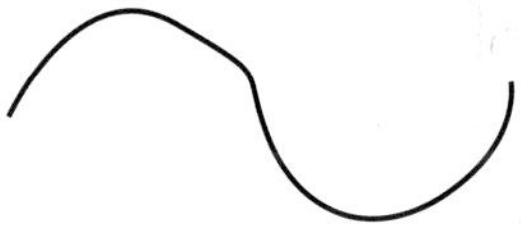

Curved line

Line

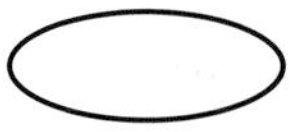

Oval

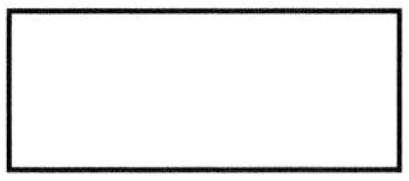

Rectangle

Shading

Square

Triangle

Glossary

algae (AL-jee) A plant without roots or stems that usually lives in water.

coral (KOR-ul) A hard substance made up of the skeletons of tiny sea animals, called polyps.

coral reefs (KOR-ul REEFS) Chains of coral where many ocean creatures live.

dorsal fins (DOR-sul FINZ) Fins on the back of a fish or water mammal.

oxygen (AHK-sih-jin) A gas in air that has no color, taste, or odor, and is necessary for people and animals to breathe.

prey (PRAY) An animal that is hunted by another animal for food.

species (SPEE-sheez) A single kind of plant or animal. For example, all people are one species.

spine (SPYNE) A sharp, rigid part of a fish.

tentacles (TEN-tuh-kuhlz) Long, thin growths usually on the head or near the mouth of animals, used to touch, hold, or move.

venom (VEH-num) A poison passed from one animal to another through a bite or a sting.

Index

Web Sites

Due to the changing nature of Internet links, PowerKids Press has developed an online list of Web sites related to the subject of this book. This site is updated regularly. Please use this link to access the list:
www.powerkidslinks.com/kgd/fish/